The Pelican Chorus

The Pelican Chorus

By EDWARD LEAR

Pictures by HAROLD BERSON

Parents' Magazine Press
New York

To Paula

King and Queen of the Pelicans we;
No other birds so grand we see!

None but we have feet like fins!

With lovely leathery throats and chins!

Ploffskin, Pluffskin, Pelican jee!
We think no birds so happy as we!

Plumpskin, Ploshkin, Pelican jill!
We think so then, and we thought so still!

We live on the Nile.
The Nile we love.
By night we sleep
On the cliffs above.

By day we fish, and at eve we stand
On long bare islands of yellow sand.

And when the sun sinks slowly down,
And the great rock walls grow dark and brown,

Where the purple river rolls fast and dim,
And the Ivory Ibis starlike skim.
Wing to wing we dance around—
Stamping our feet with a flumpy sound,

Opening our mouths as Pelicans ought,
And this is the song we nightly snort—

    Ploffskin Pluffskin, Pelican jee!
    We think no birds so happy as we!
    Plumpskin, Ploshkin, Pelican jill!
    We think so then, and we thought so still!

Last year came out our daughter Dell,
And all the birds received her well.

To do her honor a feast we made
For every bird that can swim or wade.

Herons and Gulls, and Cormorants black.
Cranes and Flamingoes with scarlet back.

Plovers and Storks and Geese in clouds.
Swans and Dilberry Ducks in crowds.

Thousands of birds in wondrous flight!
They ate and drank and danced all night.

And echoing back from the rocks you heard
Multitude-echoes from bird and bird—

Ploffskin, Pluffskin, Pelican jee!
We think no birds so happy as we!

Plumpskin, Ploshkin, Pelican jill!
We think so then and we thought so still!

Yes, they came; and among the rest,
The King of the Cranes all grandly dressed.

Such a lovely tail! Its feathers float
Between the ends of his blue dress coat;

With pea green trousers all so neat,
And a delicate frill to hide his feet.
(For though none speaks of it, everyone knows,
He has no webs between his toes!)

As soon as he saw our daughter Dell,
In violent love that Crane King fell,

On seeing her waddling form so fair,
With a wreath of shrimps in her short white hair.

And before the end of the next long day
Our Dell had given her heart away;

For the King of the Cranes had won that heart
With a Crocodile's egg and a large fish tart.

She vowed to marry the King of the Cranes,
Leaving the Nile for stranger plains;

And away they flew in a gathering crowd
Of endless birds in a lengthening cloud.

Ploffskin, Pluffskin, Pelican jee!
We think no birds so happy as we!

Plumpskin, Ploshkin, Pelican jill!
We think so then, and we thought so still!

And far away in the twilight sky
We heard them singing a lessening cry—

Farther and farther till out of sight,
And we stood alone in the silent night!

Often since, in the nights of June,
We sit on the sand and watch the moon.

She has gone to the Great Gromboolian Plain,
And we probably never shall meet again!

Oft, in the long still nights of June,
We sit on the rocks and watch the moon—

She dwells by the streams of the Chankly Bore,
And we probably never shall see her more.

Plumpskin,

Ploshkin,

Pelican jill,

We think so then and we thought so still!

The Pelican Chorus

King and Queen of the Peli-cans we,. No other birds so grand we see!

None but we have feet like fins with love-ly lea-the-ry throats and chins,

Coro -piu sostenuto.

Ploff-skin, Pluff-skin, Pe- li- can jee! we think no birds so hap- py as we!

Plump-skin, Ploff-skin, Pe- li- can jill! We think so then, and we thought so still!

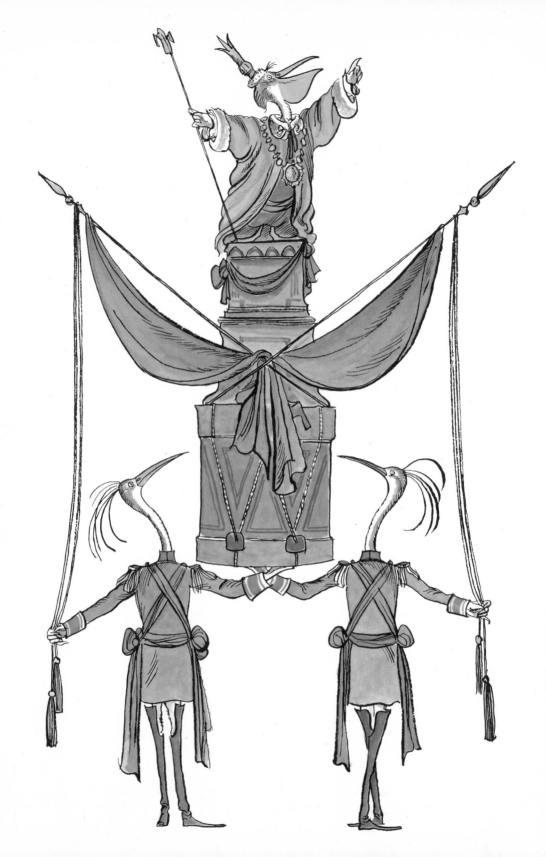